The Perfect EVE

SELF-DISCOVERY
THROUGH THE EYES OF WOMEN TODAY

ROSHAWN BURRELL

KP PUBLISHING COMPANY

ISBN: 978-1-960001-97-8 (Hardcover)
ISBN: 978-1-960001-96-2 (Paperback)
ISBN: 979-8-994090-45-9 (eBook)

Library of Congress Number: Pending

Editor: Manuscript Mender
Cover Design: Juan Roberts, Creative Lunacy
Literary Director: Sandra Slayton James

Published By:

KP Publishing Company
Publisher of Fiction, Nonfiction & Children's Books
Los Angeles · Las Vegas

Printed in the United States of America

CONTENTS

DEDICATION   *vii*

PROLOGUE   *ix*

INTRODUCTION   *xi*

Chapter 1. MODERN EVES: HOW WE'VE EVOLVED   1

Chapter 2. A MODERN REFLECTION OF EVE   5

Chapter 3. EVE IN THE GARDEN   7

Chapter 4. OTHER EVES IN THE BIBLE   13

Chapter 5. YOUTHFUL EVE (AGES 15-21)   23

Chapter 6. BECOMING EVE (AGES 22-29)   31

Chapter 7. FEARLESS EVE (AGES 30-39)   37

Chapter 8. WOKE / ENLIGHTENED EVE (AGES 40-49)   47

Chapter 9. MATURE EVE (AGES 50-59)   67

Chapter 10. SASSY EVE (AGES 60-69)   81

Chapter 11. CLASSY EVE (AGES 70-79)   93

Chapter 12. MONARCH EVE (AGES 80-99+)   101

Chapter 13. A FINAL WORD TO EVERY EVE   109

ACKNOWLEDGMENTS   *114*

ABOUT THE AUTHOR   *115*

DEDICATION

I dedicate this book to my Lord and Savior, Jesus Christ the source of my strength and purpose.

To my husband, Michael; my late mother, Alma Lee Lewis; my late grandmother, Marie Robertson; and my late aunt, BJ—your love continues to guide me. To my children, Kristian, Marcus, and Shannon; my granddaughter, Keyani; and my mother-in-love, Betty, thank you for filling my life with joy.

To my siblings—Rickey, Roberta, Cynthia, and Solo—and my sisters-in-love, Bonnie and Debbie, I love you dearly. To my cousins and sisters-at-heart—Latanya, India, Kelz, Sari, and Charmaine, thank you for always believing in me.

To my last two living aunts, Deborah and Bernice, and my uncles, Tommy and Leroy I honor your legacy. And to all my nieces, nephews, and cousins this book is also for you. May you continue to rise in faith, strength, and purpose.

You Are:

Beautiful, Victorious, Enough, Strong, Amazing, Capable, Chosen, & Creative

Illustration of The Tree of Life

NEVER ALONE AND ALWAYS LOVED!

PROLOGUE

The Perfect Eve is a collection of real-life stories today from women of all ages who have walked with the serpent. They tell stories of a time in their life when the serpent tried to lure them with a tasty, small bite of fruit. You ask, what is a serpent? It is anything not of God, anything that pulls you away from your purpose in life. The Eves recount the stories of how the serpent lied to them, tried to kill, and destroy them in any way necessary. It is our modern version of Eve.

The Perfect Eve knows she can never be perfect, but as we meet women in our daily walks of life, women who inspire, encourage, and uplift us, we can take the bits and pieces that apply to us to make a better Eve of ourselves and be the best Eve we can be.

How Could Eve Resist the Serpent?

The serpent did not come roaring or thrashing, but as a friend, perhaps even like a family member, silent, subtle, and sure. His eyes gleamed with a knowing darkness, and his words slid like silk into Eve's ear.

> *"Did God really say, 'You must not eat from any tree in the garden'?"*
>
> —Genesis 3:1 (NIV)

With that single question, her faith was shaken, and a seed of doubt was planted. Eve answered by repeating what the Lord had spoken, but the serpent pressed further, twisting truth into a lie.

"You will not certainly die," the serpent said to the woman. "For God knows that when you eat from it your eyes will be opened, and you will be like God, knowing good and evil."

—Genesis 3:4–5 (NIV)

Deceived, she longed to be like God, wise, discerning, and fully knowing. The lie took root in her heart. The fruit appeared appealing, pleasing to the eye, promising wisdom just beyond her reach. She reached. She took. And she ate.

In that moment, the whisper of the serpent became the wound of all creation.

INTRODUCTION

It was February 19, 2024. I could remember it like it was yesterday. I was getting ready for work after stepping out of my tub when it just hit me. I heard the word, Eve; Write a book about Eve. I clearly remember thinking, "What does this mean?" at 5:30 in the morning.

I thought to myself, Oh, no, not this again. It was God telling me it's time to use my creative juices and write that book we talked about. I have always felt like I am a creative person, and I know that this creative side of me comes from God. He is the one who talks to me, He gives me new ideas, and He guides me on all creative moves that I make. Now, when God tells me to move or do something, I move in two ways: quickly or sometimes like a sloth. Because I like things to be perfect, it caused me a lot of delay in writing this book. First, in my true heart, I did not want to write this book. Due to my fears and perfectionist issues, that was my delay. I like to think things over when it comes to doing God's work, because it makes me nervous and I worry about making mistakes.

Reason being, I did not want to fail my Lord and Savior Jesus Christ (My Sacrifice was what if people didn't like the book?) What if they thought, how dare she speak about the mother of all men and women? I never thought about what if they liked the book. What if this book helped women? So, I had to get out of my selfish way and realize the scripture says,

"Obedience is better than sacrifice."

—1 Samuel 15:22 (NLT)

Which is Samuel confronting Saul, asking him, Would God be delighted in his sacrifice or obedience? It says: "But Samuel replied, what is more pleasing to the Lord: Your burnt offering and sacrifices or your obedience to his voice? Obedience is better than sacrifice, and submission is better than offering the fat of rams."

I want to be obedient and be about my Father's business, which is pleasing to God. Now, when God tells me what to do, I need to do it, without second-guessing or overthinking things. There have been times when my disobedience has caused me a lot of unnecessary pain.

I have noticed that when God tells me to do something and I follow His guidance without hesitation, the results are usually beautiful and without hiccups. He always equips me with what I need, including the resources required, and He will send all the help that I need. It's okay to be nervous, do it nervously.

Like the time I created a Podcast. Without hesitation, I moved swiftly. I did what God said to do. God even sent me a specialist who was a podcast creator. It was so awesome. I am learning that it is okay to try new things. If I work on my project and assignment as God directs me, without questioning, He will work it out for my benefit. Now, if I stray away from my purpose, the pain is awful. Like the time I went back to school for my bachelor's, it was so painful. Because I moved like a sloth, I didn't move fast enough, and according to how God told me to move. So, when God told me it was time to go back to school for my master's, it was easy breezy, and I even had to maintain a 3.5 GPA. I listened, obeyed, and moved fast this time. And ladies, I want you to know it feels great just to do what God says.

This book is for all the Eves of the world; stories from all walks of women. Too often, we have heard the tale of Eve told by men, voices that speak our story but have never truly lived it or walked in our shoes. Women, we are the ones who have walked this path, this life, who have breathed life into this story with every step we take in our everyday lives. We are the Modern Eves of the world who have felt and experienced every destructive menstrual cycle, every horrible labor pain, and as we mature, every awful menopause. Let us share our story and how Eve's downfall led to setbacks that we, as modern-day Eves, overcome daily with the help of other Eves.

Before we get into *The Perfect Eve* written for women by women, can we take the time out to think about relationships that we share with women today. I enjoy sharing stories and experiences. Can you imagine not having a sister or girlfriend to share a story with? That is mind-blowing on its own, right?

As a Perfect Eve in my fifties, I've walked through a different era. My children or daughters will never have to experience some of the milestones I had to go through. I am grateful to God that they won't have to face the same experiences. I must share my experience with them so they, too, can share with other Modern Eves, so we are not repeating the mistakes of Eve.

I was a product of "busing," which took me from the inner city to the valley or suburbs to attend school, aiming to create diversity and culture among children. For me, the best thing was the exposure I got. I learned how to navigate life, thanks in large part to the knowledge I gained from attending Valley schools. What I saw and experienced was different from what they offered at my inner-city school. It wasn't bad; it just had more programs and money at their schools, allowing for more programs. Also, I didn't tell you, but in the first week of school, they were picketing outside the school as we came up to it and got off the bus. There were signs to go home; the Valley schools didn't want to accept change. They wanted us, little, inner-city kids, to go home. It did not stop the progress. The same for Eve. She was able to progress throughout life after eating the fruit.

CHAPTER ONE

MODERN EVES: HOW WE'VE EVOLVED

As Modern Eves, today's women are stronger and more capable than ever before. Unlike Eve, who had only her husband to guide her, it was about "Progressive Revelation," which means, "we have a better vantage point and more information to work with than the people in the stories of the past, like Eve." We now have countless examples to lead us through the journey of becoming the Perfect Eve, showing us how to navigate this path we call womanhood.

Eve's story in the Bible is a powerful example of the consequences of disobedience to God. However, it can also be seen as the story of a woman who missed the mark, not out of rebellion, but due to a lack of experience, connection, and support. Perhaps she missed the mark by standing alone, not walking with her husband, and allowing just enough room for the serpent to sneak in. We stand on the shoulders of incredible Eves before us, and I want you to know: this doesn't have to be our story today. It doesn't have to be your story, unless you choose for it to be. We can use stories from all women who have been through something and apply them to our lives or daily walk to help us be a better Eve.

Through the stories of Modern Eves in this book, my prayer is that you will find a few Eves that you genuinely connect with one of the Eves in this book. We no longer want the serpent to sneak up on us with his cunning, his trickery, and lead us into sin. We know we are not sinless, and we face sin in our lives. But isn't the goal to sinless to become more Christ-like?

We are blessed to be living in an extraordinary time. I'm proud to stand on the shoulders of women who came before us, those who set the bar for what we can achieve today.

So, who are The Perfect Eves? Any woman who has entered womanhood, beginning at puberty, is a perfect Eve. We are the women of today. We are Eve.

We now have the opportunity to hear from women who have faced their serpents, some they defeated, some they didn't. But they endured.

Think about it: you've faced many serpents in your life. Some tests you passed, others you didn't. But you made it through. My mother was a God-fearing woman, humble and full of grace. I witnessed her walk with God, how she treated other people and how she spoke to people, and shared His love with everyone who crossed her path. Her favorite scripture was,

> *"Delight thyself also in the LORD; and he shall give the desires of thine heart."*
>
> —Psalm 37:4 (KJV)

She didn't have an easy life. As the oldest of eleven children, she did her best with the limited resources available to her. She told me about her serpent, which was alcohol. She stop drinking and quit cold turkey, she turned to God and never looked back. She raised six children on her own and lost one child to SIDS. Through it all, she leaned on one unshakable resource: Jesus.

My grandmother, too, was a God-fearing woman. She had seen so much in her lifetime and carried a sass and toughness that came from survival. She ran away from home as a teenager in Texas, around the age of 14 or 15. As a biracial child, she endured harsh racism at a time when interracial identity was not accepted. Her faith carried her through tough times. She was more complicated than my mother, having raised children through multiple losses: four marriages, widowhood, divorce, and even the passing of some of her children. But her faith never wavered. Her serpent? Cursing. For years, she had what she called a "potty mouth." But slowly, she cleaned up her speech and began evangelizing to other women.

My Aunt BJ, who has since passed away, was also a strong God-fearing woman of faith. Her serpent was drugs. She was a talented and beautiful woman who sang and played the piano with ease. There was nothing she couldn't do. Except beating breast cancer, it really sucks. Like people say, Cancer sucks. After enduring cleaning herself off addiction, developing lost relationships with her children, friends, and family, she was always open to help feed and care for anyone in need.

The Eves of the past left us a living manual written in stories, scars, and survival. Through their trial and errors, they helped shape this book. Let's not forget them and their journeys. The serpent is still here today; we're just doing our best to stay ahead of him and his chaos. He shows up when we least expect him.

I want you to know that this book is about the relationships between women. From just casual conversations in grocery stores to heart-to-hearts on airplane flights. From stories shared at the local mall to insights exchanged over coffee. These are real experiences. Stories from strangers, friends, and family. From women willing to open up about their past, their present, and their future, about their walk with the serpent, which couldn't be anything good.

I prayed for God to give me a clear vision, to honor Eve's story, and to use it effectively as a tool for faith, healing, growth, and connection.

The Perfect Eve is a collection of stories from women of all ages and walks of life. Women have encountered a serpent or two; we know, the serpent comes to lie, kill, steal, and destroy your life. The Perfect Eve means being a better version of yourself. As women, we know we'll never be perfect. We encounter other women: mothers, sisters, daughters, friends, and from each one, we collect pieces of wisdom, strength, and truth. We gather what we need. Becoming a better Eve isn't about perfection; it's about becoming a more whole, healed, and authentic version of who God created us to be. So, when the serpent tries to attack you, we have ammunition to defend ourselves.

CHAPTER TWO

A MODERN REFLECTION OF EVE

Imagine for a moment that you are Eve, only now, it's the present day. You are a Modern Eve.

The serpent approaches you, just as it did in the Garden of Eden. He offers you the forbidden fruit, trying to tempt you, just like he did that day long ago.

But in today's world, this fruit isn't always something you can touch or taste. Sometimes, it comes in the form of an opportunity, a temptation, social media, or a decision that quietly leads us away from God's will. That "little sin," that "little white lie," it could be anything: Relationships, choices, actions, or even through thought patterns, that pulls us off the path God desires for us.

In this moment, the fruit becomes a symbol of sin; anything that distances us from God's truth and the purpose He has for our lives.

So, what would you do?

How would you respond to the serpent's whisper?

Would you resist the temptation, trusting in God's wisdom?

Or would you be drawn to something that appears pleasing, but ultimately separates you from His perfect will?

Now, The Perfect Eves will share their stories, some may tell you the age they first tasted the fruit, and how good it may have tasted until they figured out it was the serpent and his calamity. Others will tell you they tried to resist it. They will tell you how they overcame the serpent.

In this book, all the women are referred to as Eves.

Each Eve is grouped by age, given a name, and the name of the serpent's attack on her life, paired with a Scripture that reflects her journey. As stated, we know we will never be Perfect Eves, but let's take experiences from every encounter in our lives to make us better Eves.

CHAPTER THREE

EVE IN THE GARDEN

Who Is Eve? Who does the world say Eve is?

She is known as a central figure in the Bible, found in the book of Genesis. Eve is the first woman, created by God. Her story is told in Genesis, chapters 2 and 3. She is introduced as Adam's wife, the first man, and was formed from one of his ribs to be his companion. Adam called her "woman," because she was taken out of man (Genesis 2:23). Later, she was named Eve,

> *And Adam called his wife's name Eve; because she was the mother of all living.*
>
> —Genesis 3:20 (KJV)

Eve is one of the most influential women in the Bible. God gave Adam and Eve everything they needed in the Garden of Eden, with only one rule: Do not eat from the Tree of the Knowledge of Good and Evil.

But Eve was deceived by the serpent, satan, and ate the fruit from that tree. She also gave some to Adam. This act of disobedience introduced sin into the world, but it also began God's plan to redeem humanity through Jesus.

A Walk Through the Garden

Let's take a walk back through the Garden of Eden.

On that day, we find "Woman," as she was called before Adam named her, walking through the beautiful garden. The colors must have been breathtaking. Picture it: radiant yellows, deep greens, rich purples, soft browns, glowing reds, morning dew sparkling on the leaves as the light blues and oranges of the sky welcomed the day. The fruits and vegetables would have been perfectly ripe, untouched by disease or decay, nature in its purest form.

I imagine Eve walking alone, perhaps simply enjoying the beauty. After all, she had everything. What could possibly go wrong?

But just like today, even in moments of beauty, our minds wander. I've been lost in my own thoughts before, missing the presence of God's creation all around me. Mountains, birds, waterfalls, butterflies with wings of gold, orange, and sapphire, yet sometimes we're so distracted, we don't notice.

Perhaps Eve was distracted, too. Maybe she just wanted some space, from Adam, from routine, from responsibility. Then, the serpent shows up.

The Serpent Still Comes (The comparison to Perfect Eves today)

"And the Lord God commanded the man, 'You may freely eat the fruit of every tree in the garden—except the tree of the knowledge of good and evil. If you eat its fruit, you are sure to die.'" But the serpent was cunning, the craftiest of all the creatures God had made."

—Genesis 2:16-17 (NIV)

Was he watching Eve? Was he waiting for her to be alone, vulnerable, thoughtful? Isn't that just like satan, to come for us when we're emotionally isolated?

We love our alone time. But what if Eve was having one of those days? Overthinking. Questioning. Wandering. And the serpent, sly and patient, knew exactly when to whisper his lies.

Ladies, we've all been there. Why Do We Blame Her?

Let's be honest. Shouldn't we blame Adam? For years, I blamed Eve.

I'd roll my eyes and say, "Really, Eve? You just had to eat the fruit?"

I'd joke that it was her fault we have to suffer through periods, labor pains, and menopause. When things went wrong, I used to blame two people: my husband and Eve.

But today, I don't see her the same way. This book has changed that. God has matured me, and I've learned to take responsibility for my own decisions. We know God already knew what Adam and Eve would do. We can't pretend that if we had been in the garden, we would've done better. The truth? Most of us would've made the same mistake. I no longer blame my husband for my mistakes either. I've grown and matured in this area of my life.

Modern Eve and Today's Temptations.

Let's look forward to today. We are Modern Eves. We have Bibles, teachers, podcasts, and community resources that Eve never had. And yet, we still get tempted. The serpent still comes. Maybe he doesn't bring fruit. Maybe it's jealousy. Insecurity. Lust. Pride. Control. Maybe the fruit looks like a toxic relationship or a dishonest opportunity.

Would you know what to do when the serpent shows up? That's why I wrote this book. To help us see ourselves in Eve, and to grow beyond her mistake.

Personal Reflections and the Call to Obedience

God often gives me visions. Sometimes they come in dreams. But the vision for this book? It came while I was getting out of the bathtub.

Yes, wet feet, towel in hand. I heard Him whisper: "Write the story of Eve. Tell it now. In the present time." I wanted to cry. I already had another book near completion. It wasn't in my plan.

But I've learned that when God speaks, delay is disobedience.

Still, I hesitated. I doubted. I thought, "What will people think? A book about Eve? What if they mock me? What if they say I'm not qualified?" And then I realized: I was letting fear speak louder than faith. Again God has shown me that if I don't act on what He gives me, He'll hand the vision to someone else, someone willing to move now, not later. So this time, I said yes. I told Him, "Even in fear, I will write."

Eve was human, just like us. She was given free will to make her own decisions. We don't truly know why she ate the fruit. Perhaps it was because she had no one to model obedience: no mother, no mentor, no woman to say, "Girl, don't listen to that voice."

If she were alive today, we might give her a diagnosis: Anxiety. Abandonment wounds. People-pleasing. Daddy issues.

Maybe she just needed someone to listen to her.

Adam did not Cover His Wife; He Became the First Person to Shift Blame for His Own Actions.

"That woman You gave me," he said (Genesis 3:12), throwing her clearly under the bus. He deflected responsibility instead of covering his wife. And we've been repeating the blame cycle ever since.

I wrote this book to challenge those assumptions.

Every woman today, like Eve, has walked through her own garden, facing her own temptations and making her own decisions. *The Perfect Eve* contains the voices of many women; Modern Eves of all ages,

11

backgrounds, and ethnicities. They've shared their stories of how they resisted or fell into temptation, how they overcame, and how they reclaimed their worth.

And now I ask you:

- What if you were Eve?

- What fruit are you offered today?

- What has the serpent whispered to you?

The Perfect Eve is not a book of blame. It's a book of growth. It's a book about knowing yourself and knowing your God.

God told me:

"They ate the fruit. They sinned. But I redeemed them—and I will redeem you."

So walk with me. Learn with me. Let's ask the hard questions. Let's talk about the fruit, the serpent, and the God who still speaks in gardens. Eve made a mistake, but she was still chosen to give life. She was still the mother of us all.

And you, dear sister, are still part of her story.

Let's stop blaming and start becoming.
Let's stop fearing and start obeying.
Let's walk boldly, even when we're afraid.
Let's walk like Eve who know better.
Let's walk like daughters of God.

CHAPTER FOUR

OTHER EVES IN THE BIBLE: TRAILBLAZING WOMEN OF WISDOM, FAITH, AND PURPOSE

There are many other "Eves" in the Bible, women who led by example and walked faithfully into their purpose. They acted with courage, trusted God, accepted wise counsel, and embraced their callings even in uncertain times.

These women became trailblazers, not by being perfect, but by listening, growing, and walking in faith. Let's reflect on three of them: Esther, the woman with issues of blood, and Ruth.

Esther and Her Cousin Mordecai

Esther was a Jewish woman living in Persia who became queen to King Xerxes. When the king's advisor, Haman, plotted to destroy all Jews, Esther's cousin Mordecai urged her to speak to the king and intervene. It was dangerous, approaching the king without being summoned could mean death. But Esther chose to be brave.

She hosted a banquet for the king and Haman, and at just the right moment, revealed Haman's wicked plot. The king was outraged and had Haman punished. Because of Esther's courage, the Jewish people were saved, and a decree was issued allowing them to defend themselves.

Esther didn't receive this wisdom from another woman—but she listened to the maturity and experience of an elder she trusted. That's what made her so powerful: her ability to listen, weigh, pray, and act.

The Woman With the Issue of Blood

Luke 8:43–48. This story that we all know very well was a strong walk of faith. A woman having an issue of blood for twelve years, who had spent all her living (money) on physicians, could not be healed by anyone. She came behind Jesus and touched the border of his garment, and immediately her issue of blood ceased.

She clearly had faith to get to Jesus, knowing he would heal her. She kept her eyes, I am sure, on the target, which was Jesus. Can you imagine her faith walking to her target, Jesus? The walk to Jesus had to be the longest walk in her life. We know she was walking in fear; she knew she had to get to him and just touch something on him. Have you, as a woman, ever had that feeling of fear, and knew it didn't matter how scared you were? You just needed to walk in faith, trusting that nothing could stop you. And if you haven't had to take that walk yet, one day you will. As women, we all face moments where we feel like we're pushing through a crowd—bleeding in our minds, our hearts, and our faith.

Please note that God will not fail you like he did not fail her. The woman with the issues of blood is a true Eve.

This Eve is a woman who had the strongest faith. Her story is a walk of courage and strength, which she walked across that large crowd of people who could have stoned or killed her. She pressed forward, eyes focused on Jesus. We need that type of faith. Be encouraged to press forward like she did, walk in faith.

Ruth and Her Mother-in-Laws Naomi

Ruth was a Moabite woman who married Naomi's son. When her husband died, she wasn't obligated to stay with her mother-in-law, she could've returned to her family, remarried, and started over.

But she stayed. Ruth followed Naomi back to Israel, saying, "Where you go, I will go." Her loyalty was unmatched. Like many women today, Ruth chose relationship over comfort, devotion over self-interest. In Bethlehem, Ruth worked in the fields of a man named Boaz. He noticed her humility and kindness and treated her with honor. Eventually, she married Boaz, and together they had a son named Obed—who became the grandfather of King David.

Imagine if Ruth hadn't stayed with Naomi.

Imagine if she had ignored the wisdom of an older woman.

Where would King David's story be?

Ruth's life illustrates loyalty, faith, and God's perfect provision. She was a true Eve of her time.

Modern Eves Have More Than One Voice

Today, as Modern Eves, we have abundant resources, mothers, aunties, mentors, spiritual mothers, sisters, and friends to guide us. We are not alone in our decision-making. We don't have to react in fear or confusion.

Eve in Genesis didn't pause to reflect. She responded quickly to the serpent, repeating what God had said, but still allowed herself to be deceived.

What if Eve had someone around her? What if she'd had someone else's voice in her head, mentorship, wisdom, experience? Today, we do.

We can be ahead of the serpent. We can learn from the experiences of other women. That's why this book exists—to provoke conversation across generations. To help you ask the hard questions:

- How well do you really know yourself?

- What has your serpent looked like in your life?

- How did you overcome it? Or are you still facing it?

- What patterns attract the enemy toward you?

- Are you aware of your weaknesses and growing in them, or avoiding them?

Here is a Self-Check

The Perfect Eve is a reflection on your own development. It's here to help you ask, "How am I handling temptation today?"

From your early teen years to your current stage of life, how have you matured?

How did you handle the serpent when he showed up?

You'll hear stories from women of every age—real Eves who shared their insights, growth, setbacks, and victories. These women gave powerful perspectives on what it means to grow as a woman.

If You Are Eve Today

Imagine yourself as Eve, right now. Present day. Your current age.

You're married to Adam.
You live in a beautiful garden.
God has given your husband the instructions.

Some believe Eve didn't know the rules, but the Scripture shows otherwise.

> *"Of course we may eat fruit from the trees in the garden,"*
> *the woman replied. "It's only the fruit from the tree*
> *in the middle of the garden that we are not allowed to eat."*
>
> *God said, 'You must not eat it or even touch it; if you do,*
> *you will die.'"*
>
> *"You won't die!" the serpent replied to the woman.*
> *"God knows that your eyes will be opened as soon as you eat it,*
> *and you will be like God, knowing both good and evil."*
>
> *The woman was convinced. She saw that the tree was*
> *beautiful, and its fruit looked delicious, and she wanted the*
> *wisdom it would give her. So she took some fruit and ate it.*
> *Then she gave some to her husband, who was with her,*
> *and he ate it too.*

—Genesis 3:2–6 (NLT)

There is always so much controversy, and long debates around the question: Did Eve really know what God said? Let's say she did. She knew not to eat the fruit. But she lacked something we often take for granted today—wisdom, mentorship, and spiritual community.

She had no mother.
She had no mentor.
She was the first woman, facing the first temptation alone.
But What If She Had Someone?
What if Eve had paused to call on God?
What if she had asked her husband to confirm what she heard?
Where was Adam?

God had given Adam clear instruction. Why didn't he speak up? And more importantly. why do we always blame Eve more than Adam?

Modern Application

Today, if God told you not to touch the fruit, and the serpent still tempted you. What would you do?

- Would you call a trusted voice?

- Would you remember a mentor's advice?

- Would you stop to pray?

The truth is that we often want what we cannot have.

But now, we have wisdom. We have women. We have community. We have the voice of God, and the stories of those who have walked before us.

This book offers insight, but more importantly, it offers invitation:

- To reflect.

- To grow.

- To walk differently.

- To become the Eve who listens before she bites.

Every woman has a serpent moment.

The question is: How do you respond?

- Do you let him trick you?

- Do you pause and reflect?

- Do you walk away and run to God?

You have a choice. You always have a choice.

Let this chapter remind you:
You are not alone in the garden.
You have voices, wisdom, experience, and God's Spirit.
And today, you are wiser than Eve was.
Now, what will you do with that wisdom?

Her journey did not begin
or end in the garden.

Youthful Eve (15-21)

CHAPTER FIVE

YOUTHFUL EVE (AGES 15-21) LEARNING TO WALK WITH WISDOM

"Don't let anyone look down on you because you are young, but set an example for the believers in speech, in conduct, in love, in faith, and in purity."

—1 Timothy 4:12 (NIV)

This verse was initially written to Timothy; it speaks powerfully to young women. It reminds them that youth is not a limitation, but an opportunity to lead and shine for God.

She's stepping into adulthood, filled with curiosity, energy, and emotions. Youthful Eves are happy, silly, full of questions, and sometimes unsure of themselves. Some are shy, others are outgoing or reserved. All are learning how to navigate life, faith, identity, and pressure from the world around them.

Youthful Eve is beginning to make her own choices and starting to understand that her independence comes with responsibility. Let's hear from four young women who reflect the spirit and challenges of the Youthful Eve.

Monique – Age 16 (Observant)

Monique is outgoing and full of life. She loves acting, singing, and spending time with her friends. She has a close-knit group at both school and church and comes from a large family of six in total, including both parents. She's the second youngest and says her family plays a big part in her faith. Her parents often share stories about how God brought them through difficult seasons, and that has inspired her to want a closer relationship with God. She admits she doesn't know everything about Him yet, but she's trying to grow spiritually.

Her Serpent? Fearful/Heartache!

Monique says that if she were faced with the serpent, like Eve, she would call on her parents for help. She leans on their wisdom and guidance and knows she can trust them. When it comes to peer pressure, Monique is confident in saying no. She doesn't feel bad about refusing something she knows is wrong. In middle school, she used to get into trouble often. Calls to her parents from teachers were common. But she watched how her parents handled her mistakes with love and truth. Looking back, she understands they were right to discipline her.

If she ever felt tempted to eat the fruit, Monique says she would feel terrible afterward. She tries to remember how her parents would handle the situation, and she's learning to call on God in those moments, too.

Kathy – Age 17 (Bad Year)

Kathy is more reserved than Monique. She plays sports at her high school, and also competes in a travel league. Most of her friendships are with people on her team, whom she's been part of most of her life.

Kathy is close to her mother and extended family. As an only child, she's learned how to enjoy her own company and doesn't feel the need for a large group of friends.

Her Serpent? Being over Cautious!

When asked about the serpent and the forbidden fruit, Kathy is firm in her answer:

"I would not bite the fruit. I'd run like it was a stranger trying to grab me."

She admits she tends to be cautious and maybe even fearful at times, but she knows herself well. When asked about peer pressure, she answered clearly:

"I'd tell them, NO. Period!"

Kathy's strength is in her self-awareness. She knows her limits, listens to her instincts, and doesn't let others sway her easily. Her quiet courage is a reminder that even the most reserved Youthful Eve has a powerful voice.

Justine – Age 17 (Abandoned)

Justine is full of hope for the future. She's preparing for college and excited about the next chapter of her life. She plays volleyball and runs long-distance track. Outgoing by nature, she's grateful for where she is this year, especially compared to the last.

Just one year ago, Justine said she was in a very dark place. She felt like God had abandoned her. At school, her friends pulled away, and she didn't know why. At home, everything her parents said felt critical or cold. She began to believe rumors were being spread about her, though she couldn't confirm them. Her relationships unraveled, and she ended up with an entirely new friend group.

Looking back, she realizes, "Last year, I would've eaten the fruit, and truthfully, I did."

Her Serpent? The Get Back.

In her pain, she admitted she spread rumors about her old friends, even though she didn't want to. She says, "They hurt me, so I hurt them back."

It was a time of confusion, temptation, and searching. She even started questioning her Christian faith and was approached by people from other religions, inviting her to their churches. She felt overwhelmed and spiritually lost. But today, she's rebuilding.

Justine now has a new friend who introduced her to Bible study and helped her reconnect with God. She's learning from her past, and she's taking steps to become stronger, wiser, and more grounded in faith.

She's healing, making one decision at a time.

Kenzie – Age 19 (Grieving)

Kenzie had a joyful year, she went to prom, graduated, and celebrated with a big birthday and graduation party. But amid those joyful moments, she experienced a deep personal loss. Her cousin passed away unexpectedly. Kenzie was still upset with him when he died. They had argued over a silly, "he said, she said" situation, and she'd held onto that anger for a long time.

Her Serpent? Unforgiveness.

After her cousin passed, Kenzie fell into a season of anxiety and depression. She didn't know how to move forward. She questioned if she could work, go to school, or find peace again.

With the help of her therapist, supportive friends, and a loving family, she began to heal. As a Catholic, she started attending both Saturday and Sunday mass, wanting to draw closer to God.

Now, she journals to process her emotions. She writes until it becomes too much, then she goes for a walk. Little by little, she's letting go of the pain and learning to forgive herself.

Kenzie is still on her journey, but she's growing. Her Youthful Eve moment is not defined by the fruit she once clung to, but by the grace she's learning to receive.

The Journey of a Youthful Eve

Each of these young women, Monique, Kathy, Justine, and Kenzie, represents a different part of Youthful Eve's journey.

Some are walking in confidence.
Some are learning through mistakes.
Some are healing from wounds they didn't ask for.
But all of them are choosing to keep walking.

The serpent is still real, but so is the God who redeems, restores, and revives.

As we counsel our Youthful Eves, let's encourage them, give them grace and space for growth. We were once the Youthful Eves.

Connecting to Eve

Which Youthful Eve appealed to you?

_____

_____

_____

_____

_____

Do you know any Eves with similar issues?

_____

_____

_____

_____

_____

How would you support this Youthful Eve?

_____

_____

_____

_____

_____

Becoming Eve (22-29)

CHAPTER SIX

BECOMING EVE
(AGES 22-29)

"She's no longer who she was. She's Becoming Eve."

She is a woman in a different period in her life, Becoming Eve is starting to blossom, no longer who she was, but not yet who she will be. God is still writing her story. Her strength is in her surrendering, her beauty in her becoming.

> *"Being confident of this, that He who began a good work in you will carry it on to completion…"*

—Philippians 1:6

Mela – Age 26 (High-energy, Single)

Mela is outgoing, high-energy, and refreshingly honest. She works as a youth counselor and admits that right now, she'd probably eat the fruit.

"I hate to say this," she laughs, "but I like to have fun. Nothing crazy, but fun." When asked if she'd fall for the serpent's temptation, she paused. She really hates to say this, knowing her mom would not like her to say it or even act that way. She tends to walk on the wild side right now. Mela is not ready to give up her fun time.

Today, she is Becoming Eve, and she wants to know, "Where is my husband? Why am I walking alone?" "He should be with me; he's not on a phone, not watching TV. He should be walking beside me."

Her Serpent? Loneliness

Loneliness, she confessed, would be her serpent. She doesn't like being alone. She admitted that curiosity might get the best of her. "The serpent probably sounded good. I just want to know things. I've always wanted to know what's going on, at school, at home, everywhere."

As we talked, she flipped the script and asked, "Haven't you ever wanted to know something so badly you didn't even think about the risk?"

I told her I had. As a former Youthful Eve, I too would've eaten the fruit, believing I had it all figured out. But now, as a Mature Eve, I know to seek God, to pause, to pray, and to ask my husband first. Mela's honesty was refreshing. Mela's not pretending. She's learning.

Chanel – Age 26, Single (Insecurities)

Chanel is soft-spoken, analytical, and strong. She said the serpent wouldn't easily sway her, but she knows herself well enough to admit her weak spot. "Eventually, he'd wear me down. He'd hit my insecurities."

Her Serpent? Insecurities.

Chanel is sharp, educated, and knows how to guard herself. But she also knows how the enemy works. She said she'd want to ask her (hypothetical) husband before deciding to eat the fruit, but she'd also want him to be spiritually responsible.

"If he said yes, I'd still want to make the final call. But I'd want to know he's with me."

Chanel may be quiet, but clear, and her boundaries are firm. She knows her mind and her value.

Shawna – Age 27, Single (Analytical/Introvert)

Shawna is both funny and deeply introspective. She loves reading, skincare is her jam, and she spends her downtime on it. Shawna had not one but two encounters with the serpent and didn't pass the test.

In high school, she started hanging with the wrong crowd of girls who rejected parental wisdom and lived recklessly. But Shawna had something they didn't: two involved parents who prayed, paid attention, and pulled her back before it was too late. They took her phone for two years, spent time with her, and helped her recalibrate.

Her Serpent? Peer Pressure.

In college, she drifted again, partying, drinking, and smoking. Shawna was alone, without her family or support team, and missed them. She went into a period of anxiety and depression. Shawna attended a local church, but it felt foreign, and it didn't reach her. But she knew God still loved her. "When it was time to stop, I stopped. Cold turkey. "Now, Shawna mentors other young women, sharing her story and reminding them of God's love, grace, and power. Her serpent in college was separation anxiety.

The Journey of Becoming Eve

Each of these young women, Mela, Chanel, and Shawna, is in transition, entering uncharted waters; she will find her light and her way.

You Are Not:

Alone, Worthless, Forgotten, Weak,
Shameful, A Mistake, Bound, or Cursed!

Illustration of the Knowledge of Good and Evil

YOU ARE NOT ABANDONED,
YOU ARE NOT DEFINED BY YOUR SIN!

Fearless Eve (30-39)

CHAPTER SEVEN

FEARLESS EVE (AGES 30–39) BOLD, BEAUTIFUL, AND UNAPOLOGETICALLY BECOMING

Strength and honor are her clothing; she shall rejoice in time to come. She opens her mouth with wisdom, and on her tongue is the law of kindness.

—Proverbs 31:25–26 (NKJV)

A reflection of the renewal of her mind, spiritual maturity that blooms during this time of life. Discovering her true strength. "But they who wait for the Lord shall renew their strength. They shall mount up with wings like eagles; they shall run and not be weary. they shall walk and not faint."

—Isaiah 40:31 (ESV)

For Fearless Eve navigating careers, relationships, motherhood, and ministry, this verse is a promise of divine renewal and strength. Fearless Eve, bold, beautiful, and unapologetically becoming is vibrant and confident. She has a fire in her soul, a zest for life, and the courage to face her fears head-on. Fearless Eve knows what she wants and what she doesn't. She may be a firecracker, outspoken, bold, and unafraid to stand up for herself.

She's grown enough to own her past, mature enough to make better decisions, and wise enough to know she still has more growing to do.

Let's meet a few Fearless Eves who are navigating life, love, faith, and identity with honesty and strength.

Brianne – Age 33 (Protecting Herself)

Brianne is a single mother of one. She reflects on her twenties as a time when she felt unstoppable, mostly because she still lived at home and had fewer responsibilities. Life was freer and easier. Now in her thirties, she sees the shift: "Life has gotten its licks in."

She explained, "Life has been tough." Brianne experienced heartbreak, growing pains, and the pressure of adulthood. Her perspective is different now.

Her Serpent? Fear.

While some of her girlfriends still live recklessly. Brianne said, "Trying to help a 30-year-old who is dealing with consequences is scarier, as she is hyper-aware of making mistakes and feels like she doesn't know how to be an adult, trying to minimize decisions that can negatively impact her future." Some of her girlfriends are more rebellious, still wild and reckless, acting like time is on their side. Still, she is more alert now, more awake to what is going on around her.

Brianne calls herself a "super-doer Christian." She still makes mistakes, but is grounded in her faith. "I wouldn't eat the fruit on purpose," she said.

"I'm not perfect, but I've seen enough to know better."

She believes that by 30, you start to live with a deeper awareness: "You realize tomorrow isn't promised, so your choices have to matter."

Zoey – Age 31 (Resentment)

Zoey came into the conversation strong:

"I've always wanted to tell my side of the story." Growing up, people assumed she was just rebellious. In truth, she was hurt. Her parents, one Catholic and one Christian, didn't practice either faith consistently. Zoey remembers going to both church and mass, but nothing ever stuck. She remembers going to church with her dad and grandmother, and on her mother's side of the family. Zoey would go to mass with her grandparents, aunts, uncles, and cousins. She found it somewhat confusing that her parents would occasionally attend each other's churches, but it was never a regular occurrence. It was no shock to her when her parents told her they were going to divorce.

They divorced during her teenage years, and the extended family became involved. Everyone had something to say, especially about her father, and eventually, they began to hate him.

Her Serpent? Hate. Resentment. Division. (And Hate in Her Heart Towards Her Father and His Family.)

Zoey chose her mother's side because she lived with her, but the loss of her relationship with her father haunted her. On social media, she saw his family celebrating milestones without her. "They never even checked on me," she said.

College was her breaking point. She partied hard and was nearly expelled for academic issues. That's when she knew she needed something more.

Working at Starbucks opened her world. Customers offered advice, book recommendations, and encouragement. She began rebuilding herself emotionally, spiritually, and relationally.

Now, she's working on reconciling with her father, although they're not fully healed yet, but they're speaking again. Zoey says, "I see where I was wrong, too. I'm trusting that it will get better."

Linda – Aged 30, Divorced, Three Kids (Finding Her Way)

Linda is a mother of three and recently divorced. Her life has not been easy. Feeling distant from God right now, but she's trying, and feeling an off-and-on connection with Him. She just had a whole blended family, including stepchildren. Now she is starting all over. By herself.

Raised between two religions, she often felt confused. But her grandmother, a devout Christian and faithful woman, was her compass. She watched her grandmother's obedient, faithful walk, which told a different story. But God.

"I wish she were here to help me now," Linda said. She got married young, fell out of love, and became pregnant. But over time, it became all about bills and kids. Her husband worked long hours and eventually distanced himself. She never cheated, and to her knowledge, neither did he.

Her Serpent? Loneliness and Resentment.

She longed for companionship and fun, so she went out with friends while he stayed home with his games. It created space between them. They eventually divorced.

Now, Linda is reconnecting with church and herself. Her kids are in activities, she's seeing a family counselor, and preparing to love again. This time with clarity and purpose.

Tonia – Age 34, Single (Not Easily Shaken)

Tonia is disciplined and direct. She said confidently, "If God told me not to eat the fruit, I wouldn't."

Her Serpent? Being A Strong-willed Woman!

Tonia admits to being a rule follower. As a child, getting into trouble deeply affected her. Catholic, not practicing right now, but sometimes attends mass. Even now, she strives to obey authority, including God.

Tonia's not married, but knows what kind of man she wants. She is also very independent. Tonia makes her own money and runs her own business—a very independent Eve—and said, "If she had a husband, she wouldn't ask him for permission to obey God. She wouldn't ask her husband whether she should eat the fruit."

I can relate to her story of not asking her husband. In my twenties, I thought I knew everything. Now that we are older, I would ask him whether we should eat the fruit. If he had said yes, I wouldn't have eaten the fruit at this age. "My answer is No."

Tonia is a true Independent Eve. But she's also reflective and admits that in her twenties, she probably would've tried to know everything. Now, she knows better.

Tamara – Age 37, Single, College Teen Mom (Overcomer)

Tamara is a single mom, social media manager, and businesswoman. She owns her home and a rental property and focuses on building wealth. Her goal is to be a millionaire by age 40. She remembers a time in her life when she just kept going. Being a young teen mom in college was not easy. Tamara isn't currently practicing a religion and admits she's still exploring her faith. Raised in a home with both Catholic and Christian influences, she hasn't found a spiritual fit yet.

Her Serpent? Independent!

She does not want to be an independent woman. It has been her life, raised by a strong, single, independent mother and business owner. Her mother taught her to be a driver; however, she has found that independence is a lonely world. Exhaustion can come from consistently doing everything alone.

"If I were married, she said, "I'd ask my husband. Should "we" eat of the fruit? I'd want him to help make the decision. I'm tired of making every decision myself."

She knows herself well enough to say she wouldn't eat the fruit right now. But she also knows that if she had a partner she trusted, she might go along with what he chose.

Tamara longs for love, but she also knows she has work to do in herself first.

Each of these Fearless and bold women, Brianne, Zoey, Chanel, Mela, Shawna, Linda, Tonia, and Tamara are comfortable in their skin now.

- Fearless Eve is not afraid to tell her truth.

- She walked through fire, faced the serpent, and made hard decisions.

- She's not perfect. But she's powerful.

- She's not always sure, but she's always searching.

- She's not silent; she speaks with strength.

The Fearless Eves in this chapter have learned something critical: The serpent still shows up, but now, they know how to spot him.

Their honesty, resilience, and faith journey show us what it means to be a modern woman rooted in reality and reaching for purpose. Let's choose to help Fearless Eve light her fire the correct way. Helping and listening are essential, but it's not safe to play with fire if you don't know the consequences.

Connecting to Eve

Which Fearless Eve appealed to you?

_____

_____

_____

_____

_____

Do you know any Eves with similar issues?

_____

_____

_____

_____

_____

How would you support this Fearless Eve?

_____

_____

_____

_____

_____

Woke / Enlightened Eve (40-49)

CHAPTER EIGHT

WOKE / ENLIGHTENED EVE (AGES 40–49) SEEING CLEARLY, WALKING IN WISDOM

"Charm is deceitful, and beauty is passing, but a woman who fears the Lord, she shall be praised."

—Proverbs 31:30 (NKJV)

This verse celebrates the lasting beauty that grows from spiritual depth, wisdom, and reverence for God.

Woke Eve has lived long enough to see clearly and walk in wisdom.

- She discerns right from wrong.

- She's navigated relationships, challenges, and career tests— and now knows who she is. She lives in her truth and purpose.

- She no longer lives to please others. Instead, she stands firmly in self-awareness and spiritual maturity.

Let's meet the Woke Eves who have walked hard journeys and now walk wisely.

Robin – Age 44, Divorced, Two Children (Trusting in a Man of the Cloth)

Formerly married to a minister, Robin strove to be the ideal pastor's wife submissive and supportive despite feeling unseen. Robin said it was a hard decision for her to divorce her ex-husband because she still loved him, even though her husband's fruit, temptation, infidelity, and emotional distance were masked by public preaching.

She regrets not being prepared for her role and wishes she'd received mentorship on marriage and spiritual leadership.

Her Serpent? Trusting in a Man and not the Lord!

Robin said, "Of course, she would not eat of the fruit from the serpent." In the past, her relationship with her minister husband was difficult. She said it seemed like the serpent was calling the shots in her relationship. He would send all kinds of fruit her way.

Robin listened to everything her husband would say and believed him. She felt like the serpent would send women to interrupt their relationship. She felt that when her husband spoke in church, from the pulpit, he was addressing another wife, not her. The messages he would tell the church were maybe another woman he had imagined.

Robin said she was not the most mature Christian. She got the job as a minister's wife because of her husband. Looking back at their relationship, she wishes he had prepared her for the job and taught her more about the expectations of being a minister's wife. She is now learning, through reading and counseling, how to be a better person; maybe in the future, she will be okay with getting married again.

Taylor – Age 44, Single, No Children (Temptation for a Man)

Raised in ministry, Taylor's mother is an Evangelist, and her father is a Pastor. She knew Jesus inside the church walls. But the serpent whispered to her in relationships, feeding anxiety and desperation.

After a string of unhealthy romances, she reclaimed her identity. Taylor lost a "dream job" over a conflict she knew was unnecessary.

Now, she's building a better life; a job she loves and a renewed faith. She is walking with God like never before. Taylor resists the fruit, listens to God, and walks with caution.

Her Serpent? God Put the Finest Guy in Her Life!

He had an amazing smile and was so charming. He was really kind, and he knew the Bible. He was the kind of guy you take home to your mother. She started dating this guy who smelled good and checked off all the boxes. He even had his own house. He seemed like such a wonderful guy. For several months, he courted her, paying for everything. A gentleman at heart, he opened doors. Just too good to be true. Taylor met his mother, siblings, and many friends, with whom he spent time going to restaurants and having weekend barbecues. He was a great guy for about 5 to 6 months.

Now, out of the blue, he wanted to trade in his car, which was fine with her. However, he needed help with the down payment and asked her to cosign on his vehicle. She thought, It was strange; he always seemed like he had it together. Taylor was never going to cosign a loan with a boyfriend. He was not her husband. That was one of the signs from God; He showed her that she still wanted to be in a relationship with this man. It seemed like he was starting to want to impress his friends. Taylor began to notice that he wanted everything she had, like a new car. It was almost as if he were jealous of the things she had worked hard to earn. He now seemed to be at her house all the time, wanting her to purchase new things to show off to his friends and family.

Taylor explained to him that she was frugal and smart about her money. She would always pray and ask God about everything she did. However, she found herself consulting with him on everything. Taylor felt like she was beginning to be okay with all the material things, which was nothing like her. Why did she find herself consulting with this guy, who isn't her husband, and he always agreed to buy something, regardless of whether she needed it or not?

He still hadn't asked her to marry him, but he thought they should get a new home together. She said that everything he told her at the beginning of the relationship was not true; the house belonged to his father, and he had let his father stay there. His car was in a bad loan because of his credit. When Taylor started telling him no and explaining how she planned to spend her money, they argued a lot. Of course, she got rid of him by continuing to tell him no, and one day, he left.

There was another time when she fell for issues at work that she had been avoiding for a very long time. Taylor said she had been trying to avoid the drama at work, a habit she has maintained for a long time.

Finally, one of the women she worked with said something to Taylor that she considered unprofessional. The supervisors wrote her up. She said it was the serpent because, according to God, it was not a big deal, and she was to hold her peace.

As a believer and a woman of God, she could have prayed about it. Because she didn't listen to God, she received a write-up, which lasted six months. She said it was really tough, even though she didn't do it. Also, she said the employees had been trying to get her fired since the day she started working there. She signed her write-up and left that job. She has a new job, and she's also surrendering everything back to God.

Since doing so, life has been grand for her; she hasn't found anyone yet, and she is okay with it. God will send her a husband and children if she wants one. She has a better job now, with great benefits, pay, and opportunities for promotion. The serpent struck her in two ways: insecurity with a man and a lack of faith in God. Her serpent, not trusting the lord, believed this job was her dream job, but it wasn't. (She had to seek God). Meditating on Exodus 14:14, *"The Lord shall fight for you, and you shall hold your peace."* I love it when God interrupts my thoughts to remind me that this battle is not mine, but his.

Alicia – Age 48, Divorced, Two Children (Betrayed)

Alicia felt she had "it all" until betrayal and heartbreak shattered her marriage. For the past two to three years, she has suffered in silence. Confused and feeling alone.

Though she once believed herself picture-perfect, pain made her eat fruit she now regrets. But today, Alicia is renewed—reborn, forgiven, and reconsecrated. She deepened her faith, rededicated her life to Christ, and found peace.

Her Serpent? Betrayal and Unforgiveness, Causing Her to Crash Out!

Now, she remains mindful: she would not eat that fruit again. Alicia felt like she was 25 years old again; she was living her best life, partying and not having a care in the world. Her divorce made her so unhappy. Alicia is the best mom to the children that she could be. She feels a minor depression has set in.

Alicia is honest and transparent. After her divorce, she didn't know what to do. But to eat of the fruit. She could not see clearly, and she understood the serpent's assignment was to come in and destroy her. Alicia was living out of pain and an unforgiving heart. She knew better. Betrayal got the best of her. And unforgiving him was wrong.

She has since forgiven him, rededicated her life to Christ, and was re-baptized. She is working on her daily devotions and reading her word.

Alicia is now active in her church and hasn't gotten back with her ex-husband, saying it's okay; God is her husband for now.

Alicia focused first on building a better bond with God and explained that Eve was not supposed to eat the fruit, just as she was not supposed to "wild out." However, God gives us grace and repentance. She wants to do what God said, but she was stuck in a difficult situation.

As of today, she is back to partying and wilding out. She doesn't see how she can escape this place. She is sad, but really enjoys being with someone. So, until that day, Alicia said, "she will continue to do for herself." (She knows it's wrong, but so is the situation she was given.) Right now, she works and takes care of herself, and she doesn't have to worry about her grown children.

Elizabeth – Late 40s, (Long-Term Partner)

I met Elizabeth in Cancun, and we became friends immediately. She was one of the nicest people who was working at the hotel resort where I was staying. We had coffee at the resort, and she told me she had a long-term boyfriend who was buying a house with land for a farm in Cancun.

I asked her what the delay was with getting married to him? Elizabeth was not sure. She's a non-practicing Catholic, and because she and her boyfriend were living together, the church would not approve their marriage. Elizabeth wants to get married, have kids, and be married, but is waiting for him. She didn't fully understand the question, but said she knows God wants her to be married, and that it is a commitment. Because they're not married and Catholic, family expectations weigh heavily on her.

Elizabeth recognizes the tension, waiting, and wondering if staying unmarried is walking out on morals or misaligned with her calling. She is happy with him but longs to get married.

She knows what she should avoid.

Her Serpent? Waiting for a Man to Ask Her to Marry Him!

She's simply searching for clarity and courage.

Jayme – Age 48, Divorced, Three Children, Caregiver and Mother (Loneliness)

Jayme is a believer. She struggles with this story because she feels alone right now. The serpent could get her into a state of loneliness. She knows that if the serpent were to come up to her and ask her to eat of the fruit, she would. It would be because she would love to be in a relationship with a man. Jayme would like to be married again. Men have always been her weakness. It has not always been easy for her; she believes she has daddy issues and is almost overcoming them.

Jayme is dealing with those issues much better now. Her father has since passed away. She states one thing she knows more than anything is that her heavenly Father will always bring her through.

Today, with the knowledge she has gained from childhood until now, she would not eat the fruit because God said so. When Jayme was younger, her upbringing and the history with her father and ex-husband might have led her to eat the fruit. Due to insecurities and unresolved issues with her father, the serpent could have easily deceived her. She mentioned that life has its ups and downs, and in certain moments, she might give in and eat the fruit, while at other times, she would resist.

Her Serpent? Loneliness!

She longs for partnership and intimacy, sometimes feeling driven to compromise her values for connection.

Her father's absence, combined with marital betrayal, intensified this hunger.

Today, she stands firm, knowing her Heavenly Father will provide.

If the serpent came to her today, she would resist—armed with spiritual grounding and self-awareness.

Terry – Age 40, Married, Stepmom (God has Consequences)

Terry is married and has no kids of her own but has a stepchild. She is a bold, spunky, and witty Eve. Terry claims no one will ever hurt her again.

Her Serpent? No One Will get Over on Her Again!

She has seen way too many things, and she now knows how to navigate life. She speaks with confidence and poise; she doesn't hold back her words. Terry was a woman small in stature, but strong and powerful in words, stated that if God had told her not to eat of the tree of knowledge, she would not have eaten the fruit.

At age 40, she boldly states that not listening to God has significant consequences, including getting into trouble for your actions. "Your consequences can land you in jail," she states. Terry is a small woman who would not want to go to jail; she would not make it in prison because she could not protect herself in that environment. For that matter, Terry would not want any legal issues arising when people do not follow God's laws.

Because of the type of person Terry is, she would surely consult with her husband. She likes to consult with her spouse about everything, even the little things, always asking him for his advice. When she was single, it was different; she still found herself questioning her sisters about what they would think.

Terry prides herself on discernment and clear boundaries. She says unequivocally: she will not eat the fruit. She knows obedience matters—not just spiritually, but practically too.

Her father's absence, combined with marital betrayal, intensified this hunger.

Annette – Age 49, Remarried, Five Children, Seven grandchildren (She Stayed Too Long)

She is 49 years old and holding on firmly to her forties. Not ready to enter her fifties yet! Annette was previously married to a husband she was not equally yoked with. She felt she had done everything for her previous husband. Annette never felt like she was enough for him. She always had strong faith and believed God would fix him, and he would stop being a cheater and manipulator.

Her Serpent? Not listening to God in Her Relationship with Ex-husband!

He told her many times to leave him when her children were younger, but now that they are grown, it's caused issues with the kids, who are taking sides and deciding which parent to believe. It's better now. In the beginning, the children did not understand, but God.

Her parents have been married all her life, so she has seen a great example of a great marriage.

Annette is now remarried, and her husband is several years younger than she. In this new relationship, they are like teenagers. Always having a great time. Her new husband is a man truly sent from God. He is a Christian, kind, and patient. He leads and is the head of his household. He is a fantastic grandfather to the grands, even though he has no children of his own, he is such an incredible man of God.

Now, with a new vision, she says she would not eat the fruit. If God told her to follow His word and rules, she would. Her past marriage, divorce, and the traumas associated with bad breakups and development caused her to discover herself. Of course, in her first marriage, she would have eaten the fruit because she wanted to please him.

It could be one of the reasons the crafty serpent would have had her eat the fruit. Not now, but she wouldn't have consulted her previous husband. Why would she have consulted with him? Trust should be a big part of their relationship, and she had none in him. He would have probably told her to eat the fruit. He was just like that.

Now with an awareness of God and a new lease on life. If the serpent were now to ask her, "Would she eat of the fruit?" She would say, "Surely not," with a hint of doubt, then ask her husband, "Should we eat of the fruit that God told us not to eat?" She asks her hubby everything now. What should we eat for dinner? Does this meat look good? She is now mature, and her development has improved significantly.

Her first marriage ended in emotional exhaustion and spiritual disconnection. Annette stayed too long, believing God could fix it—until the serpent proved too strong. Happier now and restored in a spiritually aligned marriage, she consults her husband on life's decisions.

She knows the cost of ignoring God's warning—and refuses to repeat it.

Sarah – Age 42, Nurse & Soul Survivor (Trust Issues)

For the past 12 years, Sarah has been a single mom, raising three kids. She left her husband in a hurry one day when he was not home. She was 8 months pregnant and did not look back. The Serpent in her life at this time was her ex-husband (trust issues). He would lie to her. Tell her random stories for no reason once they were married.

Sarah is a nurse, and when she met him, he was such an amazing guy. He had it going on. His resume checked off all the boxes. She had no children, and he had only one child from his previous marriage. So how could there ever be anything wrong with him? Successful job with good benefits. Very handsome. So why did he start changing? She skipped over the details with him. She really didn't explore the telltale signs that he had a type of woman. For some reason, they all look alike. Second, they were all nurses and independent with their own money.

His character flaws were issues that he excelled in sales, and he was an excellent salesman at his previous job. So, meeting and dating her, he sold her a lemon. He made himself out to be the best guy in the world. It turned out he was the lemon. The relationship with that serpent was horrible; he tried to take the home that her mother had given to her. He also tried to take custody of their three children. She could not take it anymore. He was verbally abusive and made her think she was crazy. He was a narcissistic person. He had her friends and family believing every story he told them that she was not a good mother.

The judge believed she was an unfit mother. She feels people have not always been kind to her. She wants to be married again; however, now she has trust issues with men and women. Now a new believer, coming from a Catholic background, she still wrestles with trust and God's voice. But as a baby Christian, she is the happiest she has ever been.

If the serpent tempted her today, she'd be uncertain.

Her Serpent? Trust Issues!

Sarah feels that if the Serpent were to come up to her right now and ask her to eat of the fruit, she would be confused, not knowing what to do or what direction to take. She wants to do what's right, but she's not sure how.

Sarah is searching for clarity and finds peace in growing closer to Christ. (Update today: Sarah is back in court with her ex-husband, who is lying and still trying to get full custody of their three children.) Let's keep her lifted up in your prayers.

Heather – 49 years old, Married for 29 years, 3 children (Didn't Have a Voice.)

Today, knowing what Heather knows, she would not eat of the fruit, but baby, in the past, she said she would have the serpent eat out of her hand. In her twenties, she was wild and had a roller coaster of a time. Wild in her youth, Heather lived a life of extremes—driven by trauma, rebellion, and control.

Her Serpent? Hurt!

Her early years shaped her into someone who sought power. But God's grace softened her. Now wiser and humbled, she knows her boundaries—and she answers no voice but his.

She was really trying to figure it out. Some of the reasons she was wild in her twenties were her upbringing. Coming into her own in her thirties with her last baby was different after 9 years with no babies; she turned into another person, and her life changed. Sarah said she was always in control. She's learning that she doesn't always need to be in control. She can watch, learn, and wait. Being physically and mentally abused and not allowed to speak as a child was no laughing joke.

No voice calls her to be off the chain once she was freed from childhood abuse. She was free to do as she pleased. She is now working on dealing with these emotions; she is a child of the foster care system. Yes, her caregiver was a family member, but they were mean. It means if that parent was having a bad day, it was a spanking for her. Growing

61

up, waiting for the day to be liberated, a lot of it made her unapologetic now, regardless of her voice. No one can push her around (or put the baby in the corner she laughed.) She now firmly advocates for families, making her voice known. She will never be silent again. Now that she is fully aware of him, he would be deceived.

Sylvia – 48 years old, Married, Three Children, and a Bonus Child, One Grandbaby (Grief)

Sylvia has always been a believer in Christ and has always trusted in His word until one of her children passed away three years ago. Now she has been questioning everything. How could this happen? Her child was such a good child, never got into trouble, and was always the voice of reason. She was proud to be this child's mother. Before the child passed away, she was an outgoing person. Now, Sylvia is quieter and more reserved.

Sylvia couldn't understand and went into a deep depression; she had never felt this low in her life. There was nothing that anyone could say to her or do. Not therapy, not God. It took her over two years to come out of severe grief. She had to reclaim her faith walk back with God.

Sylvia is healing now with God, therapy, writing in her journal daily, and medication.

Her Serpent? Grief! (Caused Her not to See Clearly.)

Sylvia lost her way and doubted God, and now understands 2 Corinthians 5:21: *"I am the Righteousness of God in Christ Jesus."*

Sylvia is reclaiming her life and has returned to work part-time, repairing a relationship that was lost when she was dealing with depression.

Alicia, Jayme, Terry, Priscilla, Annette, Sarah, Sylvia, and Heather share two truths in this chapter: Forgiveness and walking by faith. Woke/Enlighten Eve sees the serpent clearly. She's been hurt, healed, and transformed.

- She doesn't just talk faith—she lives it.

- She is seasoned but still growing.

- She understands evolution doesn't end; it refines.

The serpent still shows up—but now, she knows better. Wisdom, forgiveness, love, and embracing the future should be her Joy.

Connecting to Eve

Which Woke/Enlighten Eve appealed to you?

_____

_____

_____

_____

_____

Do you know any Eves with similar issues?

_____

_____

_____

_____

_____

How would you support this Woke/Enlighten Eve?

_____

_____

_____

_____

_____

Every Eve carries a story shaped by choice, courage, and calling.

Mature Eve (50-59)

CHAPTER NINE

MATURE EVE (AGES 50–59) WISDOM WORN WITH GRACE

"Even to your old age and gray hairs I am he,
I am he who will sustain you.
I have made you and I will carry you.
I will sustain you and I will rescue you."

—Isaiah 46:4 (NIV)

A beautiful promise of God's faithful presence—no matter the season or the change.

Mature Eve has acquired wisdom. She has weathered many storms; she is worn with grace. According to Webster's Dictionary, the word "mature" describes a stage of completeness where one has reached full development. For Eve in her 50s, maturity means a life seasoned by experience, refined by struggle, and graced with wisdom. She's been through life's ups and downs: the loss of loved ones, broken relationships, health shifts, financial pivots, and changing roles. And yet—she is still standing, beautifully, boldly, and wiser than ever.

Mature Eve no longer lives to please others. She has outgrown insecurity and walks confidently in her identity. Menopause might have knocked on the door, but she answered it with resilience. The noise of the world no longer sways her; she hears the voice of God louder now than ever before.

Let's meet these wise, wonderful women.

Carry – Age 51, Separated, Five Children, Three Grandchildren (Stayed too Long)

Carry was married for 22 years to a minister struggling with mental illness. She stood by his side for decades, always supportive, always putting family first, the kind of wife who makes his plate before her own, feeding the children and holding everything together. But his refusal to acknowledge his mental health needs led to a breaking point. He lost his church, and the weight of that loss began unraveling everything.

Her Serpent? Guilt and Feeling Sorry for Her Husband!

Now separated and at peace with her decision, Carry walks with deep faith. She says she would never eat of the fruit—not in any capacity. Of course, in her younger years, she tasted the fruit like every other woman. Her maturity lies in knowing when love means letting go. Update: She has since divorced him, he has moved out, and she is now the head of the household and reconnecting with God.

Everything she thought she had lost in the past, she has regained with fullness. She continues to trust God; she continues to sing and dance his praises, for he is God, and His Mercy is everlasting. She is full of peace.

Latrice – Age 53, Married 30+ Years, Three children, One Grandbaby (Non-recognizable)

Married for over 30 years to her high school sweetheart, she has three children. Confident, wise, and fiercely protective, to know her is to love her. Latrice is rooted in faith. But if you'd met her between the ages of 15 and 26, you might not recognize the woman she is today. Those were her wild years marked by hustle and self-preservation. She had to make sure she always made money so that she would never go hungry, as she did when she was a child. Raised in a home where scarcity was common, she vowed never to go without it again. That drive fueled her early independence.

Her Serpent? Scarcity! (She Would Never go Without!)

Latrice learned to work very hard. Purchase the things she liked. Things that were for her family and herself. Probably things that she didn't have in life, so she made it happen for herself. A self-starter and go-getter. She would find a way to make things happen, buying her first home on her own. She admits it now with a smile, but back then, she was headstrong, fierce, and determined to live life on her own terms. If the fruit had been offered to her during those years, she says she would have eaten without any hesitation. Would have been having a party

69

with the fruit and offering him some. Of course, in her younger years, her husband would have eaten some, too.

She attributes being off the chain to her upbringing. As the eldest, she stepped into a mommy role early on, raising her siblings while still trying to figure out who she was. She raised her sibling before she was a mother to her own children. As she was figuring out life with her husband, being married young, responsibility shaped her before she even had time to enjoy her own youth. Being a mother early in life wasn't easy, but she does this job so well now. It was instilled in her as a young lady, and now she is the mother of the motherless. Always looking out for women and children without parents or guidance, she now seeks to help them however she can. Providing them with food, shelter, and daily essentials. God did this for her, and she surely can give back to others.

Through it all, Latrice carried a strength that was both seen and unseen. And even in her lowest moments, she never forgot how to call on God. When trouble came, when she felt overwhelmed or unseen, she lifted her voice, and He answered. Every time. Now, she has a testimony of grace, peace, and forgiveness that supersedes everything. She may have stumbled in her youth, but today she walks in wisdom as a mature Eve and would never eat the fruit again if offered to her by a serpent. And she knows exactly who to run to—because the God who was with her then is still the same God who walks with her now.

Sonya – Age 52, Married, No Children (Not a Damsel in Distress)

Elegant, intelligent, and poised, Sonya carries herself with quiet strength. She is educated, works in the wellness and healthcare field, and carries herself with such intelligence and grace. Sonya is well-put-together and so sharp. To see her is to know that she is poised and unshakable. In her younger years, people mistook her gentleness for weakness, especially the men. They felt she needed to be rescued. They assumed she needed saving. But she knew better. Sonya was not a damsel in distress. She has always been aware of what she does and how to do it.

She knows this should not be the case, but she was able to save herself.

Her Serpent? Handling Life's Temptation!

Even in her twenties, when she was newly married, she believed she could handle life's temptations on her own. Back then, she wouldn't have consulted her husband about eating the fruit, not out of defiance, but from confidence in her own discernment.

Now, she sees deeper. Today, she recognizes the serpent's disguise instantly. She walks in step with God, rooted in discernment, not fear. Sonya doesn't ask anymore; she knows the fruit is never worth it. Fast forward to now, she has discernment, awesome ears to identify the serpents, and she is well able to note his distractions.

She recognizes the serpent because she yields and walks with God. She no longer needs to ask her husband, for the wisdom Sonya has gained was not born of capability alone, but cultivated through discernment.

With years behind her and the Spirit within her, Sonya walks differently. She doesn't just face temptation; she recognizes it. She hears the hiss behind smooth words, sees the disguise behind good intentions. She doesn't entertain distractions dressed as opportunity. Why? Because she walks closely with God. Her discernment is not rooted in fear, but in intimacy with the father.

Ariel – Age 53, Married, No Biological Children (Overthinker)

Ariel has a mother's heart, even without biological children. Surrounded by nieces, nephews, and the children she helps raise, her love flows freely. Mature, perhaps even too mature. Ariel often struggles with overthinking.

If offered the fruit today, Ariel admits she might still eat it, not out of ignorance, but because she would think herself into confusion. Over-analyzing has affected both her work and home life. Although she values her husband's perspective, Ariel knows she'd ultimately make the final decision.

Her Serpent? Unforgiven/Trust Issues!

Honest, raw, and deeply reflective, Ariel acknowledges that she started late in life and is now determined to grow. "Fifty-five," she says, "will be my year of breakthrough." Her need to get everything right, checking every box twice—has sometimes worked against her. At work, that same overthinking has led to disciplinary write-ups, despite her being skilled and highly capable. At home, the pattern continues and feels even heavier.

Aware that the serpent was cunning and persuasive, Ariel believes she could be deceived just as easily. In her family, manipulation feels familiar; relatives often draw her into situations she'd rather avoid. Though she resists, their tactics leave her uncertain about how to respond, and that uncertainty frustrates her.

Ariel treasures her marriage and admits she would likely consult her husband about eating the fruit but ultimately make her own choice. "At the end of the day," she said, "it will be my decision on what I decide."

During our interview, Ariel's vulnerability was evident. Her story, shaped by a difficult upbringing, came straight from the heart. She recognizes that those early experiences led her to hold back in life, but now she's ready for change. As our conversation unfolded, she asked many thoughtful questions, double-checking each one. Beneath the insecurity was a woman earnestly seeking growth and believing that her fifty-fifth year would mark a new beginning.

Janet – "Fifties," Married, No Children, (Fiery Temper)

Janet is finding her rhythm in her fifties. Once a woman without a clear identity, she's now rooted in prayer, connection, and spiritual growth. The Holy Spirit guides her steps, and she hears God more clearly with each passing year.

Her past Serpent? A Fiery Temper, Promiscuity, and Alcohol!

She was a fighter—physically and verbally. But God has softened her. Today, she walks in peace and transformation. So, when does the serpent show up now? She sees him coming from a mile away.

Lisa – Age 52, Married 17 Years, No Children (Immaturity)

Lisa is a woman of grit. Raised Baptist but disconnected from the denomination, she lived most of her life by her own rules. Her twenties and thirties were full of partying, drinking, and fighting. She didn't just eat the fruit—she danced with the serpent.

Her Serpent? Drinking!

Her transformation came late, but it came. Now in her fifties, Lisa's reflective and sober—physically, emotionally, and spiritually. If the serpent came to her today? She'd slam the door in his face.

Kim – Age 58, Divorced and Remarried, Three Grown Children (Emptiness)

Kim describes her younger self as a "heathen," laughing now, yet fully aware of the pain it took to get here. Raised in poverty, she was determined to escape it. Beauty and charm became her currency; men were often the means to gain the gifts, attention, and validation she craved.

Her serpent/Manipulation? (Using Others to Fill the Emptiness Within.)

Compliments fed her confidence, but the satisfaction never lasted. When marriage came, love was something she didn't understand. The relationship revolved around her needs; giving was foreign to her. The serpent whispered that it was never truly about her husband.

Kim saw herself as the prize, forgetting that marriage calls two people to become one. Reality hit hard when her husband walked away and didn't look back. That loss brought her to her knees before God. Surrender replaced pride, and repentance birthed transformation.

Today, Kim is remarried to a man of faith who has shown her what true love looks like. The woman who once chased validation now walks in peace and purpose. The serpent had her once, but not anymore.

Dorothy, 55 years old, Never Married, No Children, (Unfair)

Dorothy said that she may have missed her mark around marriage and children. She may be a spinster for life. Dorothy remembers a time in her youth when she was so picky about men and relationships. A strong, educated woman, she thinks this has always scared off men.

Her Serpent? Feeling Life not Being Fair!

Dorothy has struggled with bipolar disorder and depression issues for years since the loss of her best friend, her mother, who was her everything. Her mother supported and guided her. Gave her all the advice in the world, listened to her life stories, and never judged her. That was a significant loss to her; she feels she has never recovered or met another person like her mother.

She has a relationship with God. It feels like a conditional relationship; sometimes He is present with her, and sometimes she feels like it's just her against the world. Alone, she knows she needs to trust more in God and lean not on her own understanding. She is trying to work through things and feels she is not 100% whole. Praying to God, knowing one day she will get there. Yes, she has been in therapy for years and does read her Bible.

For: Carry, Latrice, Sonya, Ariel, Janet, Toni, Lisa, and Kim. This chapter of Mature Eve's life isn't about regret—it's about redemption. It's about finally arriving at a place where she knows:

She doesn't need to eat fruit. She has already tasted grace.

Mature Eve knows who she is. She's fallen and risen. She's lived and learned. No longer needs validation from man, nor permission to walk in purpose. She doesn't chase fruit that looks good but leads to destruction.

She knows the serpent's voice—and the voice of God. Let's walk in purpose alongside Mature Eve, being ready to finish our assignment.

Connecting to Eve

Which Mature Eve appealed to you?

_____

_____

_____

_____

_____

Do you know any Eves with similar issues?

_____

_____

_____

_____

How would you support this Mature Eve?

_____

_____

_____

_____

_____

*Every woman stands
at a turning point.*

Sassy Eve (60-69)

CHAPTER TEN

SASSY EVE (AGES 60–69) GRATEFUL, GROUNDED, AND GRACEFULLY BOLD

"Likewise, teach the older women to be reverent in the way they live... Then they can urge the younger women to love their husbands and children, to be self-controlled and pure..."

—Titus 2:3–5 (NIV)

A cornerstone scripture honoring the powerful role of older women as spiritual mentors and guides.

Sassy Eve is grateful, grounded, and gracefully bold. She is full of spice and wisdom. She's lived through the seasons, survived heartbreak and loss, witnessed generational change, and still walks with her head held high. At this stage, she's grateful to be alive, with a little edge, because she's earned it. She's not here to sugarcoat the truth, but to serve it with grace, laughter, and sass.

Seasoned and sharp, and she knows who she is. She'll offer you advice, if you're open to receiving it. And if you're not? She's still okay. Because Sassy Eve doesn't need validation, she walks in her truth.

Michelle – Age 67, Divorced, Two Children, Three Grandchildren (Non-negotiable)

Michelle is every bit the definition of Sassy Eve. She is divorced and a proud grandmother, and now partly retired from a long career as a community event planner. She is fully content.

"I can see the serpent in my peripheral vision," she says with a wink. "The serpent doesn't sneak up on me anymore," Michelle said.

She has had her fair share of serpents who have tried to get her to bite the fruit. Michelle was raised in an era when grace and poise were non-negotiable. "We were always ladies," she recalls. "We carried ourselves accordingly. We could not do a lot of ungodly things."

Her Serpent? Old Fashioned Beliefs!

Michelle's upbringing, surrounded by family, brothers and sisters, and watchful neighbors, kept her grounded and out of trouble. She lovingly refers to her husband as her "Crazy Adam." Her ex-husband was an old-fashioned man. His old-fashioned views and controlling expectations strained their union. She gave the relationship her all and never wanted to get divorced. Her marriage was something she really wanted to maintain. Michelle believed it was always displeasing to God to get a divorce; She now knows better. She doesn't blame the serpent entirely, but in the end, it was simply not meant to be. However, she does acknowledge that subtle spiritual warfare crept in.

"That's what the devil does," she reflects. "He comes to destroy families, and for sure, he destroyed hers. But today, Michelle is sharp, self-aware, and wouldn't come within ten feet of that fruit.

Kia – Age 68, Married 42 Years, Three Children, Five Grandchildren (Bossy)

Kia is strong-willed and open-hearted. Known affectionately as "Auntie" by many beyond her family, she has a nurturing spirit and a fierce presence.

She admits she still wrestles with the serpent—especially when it comes to being bossy. Raised as the oldest in a large family, she took on a motherly role early. Being in control became her default.

Her family often teases her: "Mom, you can't always be right!" Her response? "Well, someone has to be."

Her Serpent? Control and Letting Go!

Despite the tension, Kia loves deeply and gives generously. Her faith is solid—built on a transition from Catholicism to Christianity after years of unanswered questions.

"I love my faith," she says. "But I'm still growing," Kia admits that the serpent still tempts her in areas of selfishness and stubbornness. She's even considering counseling, saying, "Maybe it's time to work on what's been holding me back." That's the essence of Sassy Eve: Aware, evolving, and unafraid to tell the truth. Her serpent? Selfishness and being bossy.

Kia works for herself and is always in control, as she told me. She said her faith is very strong. She hates to say that, but it is the truth. Kia's set in her ways, and sometimes she wants to do her own thing. Kia said she is a Christian now and loves her faith. It is why her faith is so strong; she reads her Bible and reads a daily devotional. Being raised as a Catholic was different. Kia would see the priest often for issues that would occur, having many questions about being Catholic that she didn't understand. Kia never felt like she received the answers she needed. So, one day, her friends took her to church, and she loved it. She never looked back. Kia mentioned that the Catholic church is very structured, which she prefers. She did fight a lot with the questions and concerns surrounding being catholic. As a Christian, she now has a resource to answer any questions: Her Bible.

Kia is being honest, saying she doesn't have many friends. Most of the time, her husband and children argue with her or complain, telling her she is too mean. They tell her, "Mother, you cannot always be right." She thinks the serpent would get her on selfishness and being bossy, which is something she learned growing up and never lost. She said she has a caring and giving heart.

Kia was the oldest child in a time when both her parents had to work, leaving her to watch her siblings. She is used to giving orders and telling people what to do, not the other way around. It's when she encounters all her problems that they try to tell her how to do something. Kia really wants to do better, and she has tried so many times to change. She is aware that the serpent is creating these problems. Kia is thinking about going to counseling. She said her kids tell her she is too old to act the way she acts.

Shelly – Age 65, Married 40 Years, Blended Family of 5, Seven Grandchildren, Four Great-Grands (Emotional Absence)

Shelly is the Monarch of her family, a retired social worker, and her home is a sanctuary where everyone—biological or not—is welcome. "They're all my kids," she says with a smile.

Growing up in a large, community-focused family, she learned early the importance of love and protection. But as a young woman, she looked for love in the wrong places—chasing connection due to the emotional absence she witnessed in her parents' marriage.

"I never saw my parents hug or kiss," she says. "So I sought that affection elsewhere."

Eventually, God placed a good man in her life—one she almost let go because he seemed "too good to be true." Now, 40 years later, they model love openly for their children and grandchildren.

Her Serpent? (Was Rooted in Longing for Love! But Her Testimony is Steeped in Grace.)

Her life echoes Philippians 4:13: *"I can do all things through Christ who strengthens me."*

Shelly is a 65-year-old who is raising a blended family of five children, seven grandchildren, four great-grandchildren, and numerous nephews and nieces. She believes it's crucial to acknowledge this because, to her, everyone is like a child.

Family members and friends are always family at her house, or she is at their house. Because she is the monarch of her family, everyone goes to her for advice.

Shelly grew up in a large family, where her father and mother welcomed everyone into their home. They grew up during a time when the neighbors were a community. She said everyone kept a watchful eye on each other. There was a local neighborhood watch sticker on the window of her home growing up, and they just watched out for everyone.

She said the serpent was in the past, and that he would have gotten her because she was promiscuous when she was younger. Shelly didn't know she was looking for love in all the wrong places.

Seeing her parents' relationship was none and void. It was apparent they were married, but, in those days, there was no public affection. They slept in the same room, had many children, and the father worked a lot. Her mother was the homemaker. She doesn't recall seeing her parents kiss or hug.

Shelly and her husband love each other. This way, the kids will know it's okay to show love in front of their children and grandchildren. She believes that if she had seen more of this in her father and mother, she wouldn't have sought love from young men. Not too many guys, but enough before she got married. Shelly said she almost let her husband go; she thought he was too good to be true. But God. He rescued her, saving her from the disbelief that a man was all she needed.

Sophia – Age 63, Separated, Three Children, Three Grandchildren (Played by the Rules)

Sophia has always played by the rules. A woman of integrity, she worked hard to hold her family together, even when her husband changed due to illness, mental or otherwise.

Her Serpent? Trusting in People!

Sophia said that she knows God will not fail her, but His children are another subject.

Her husband walked away from her, the children, his job, and their life. But she stayed. She paid the bills, the mortgage, kept the home, and raised the kids. The kids are grown, and they are in a heated divorce. He wants more than half of everything. She knows God will bring her through these storms just like he always does.

"If the serpent had tried me then," she says, "I would've said no. And if my husband wanted to eat the fruit, I would have told him to eat it alone." Update: She is still in court, fighting her way through this nasty divorce. Please keep her in your prayers.

Sophia has nothing to prove. She's lived honorably and still walks in faith. Knowing God will bring her through this process. She will not be shaken or moved by anything around her.

Erica – Age 67, Divorced (Unshakable)

Erica says today she knows better than to allow the serpent to trick her. Her season of uncertainty stretched from age 35 to 45. She was divorced, lost, and vulnerable.

Her Serpent? Uncertainty!

That was 10 years of her life when she felt the serpent knew her weaknesses, and it seemed he knew her every move, as if he were trying to guide her and pulling her strings because she was lost, afraid, and lonely. But by 45, and thank God for 45 renewals of her life, she had found her way again. Letting God align her step. Feels so much better when God is leading you and not the serpent.

Now, she's unshakable. "God is within her; she shall not be moved." Psalm 46:5

Mindy – Age 65 (Seeks Validation)

She believes everything is in God's hands, His word is truth, and it is what she walks by today. About 10-15 years ago, she didn't always feel His word was truthful.

Her Serpent? Trust!

At age 25-30, Mindy would have eaten the fruit—no hesitation. Mindy would have grabbed that fruit and asked for seconds. She was a mess back then; rebellion ruled life and her decisions. Mindy was a people pleaser. The serpent can trick you if you lack discernment. Today, as a knowledgeable individual no longer needing to please people, she's rooted in truth.

Mindy says now, "Devil, you are a liar."

She no longer seeks validation from friends. She no longer follows crowds. Her discernment is sharp, and her confidence is divine.

Abby – Age 68, Married 50 Years (A Gift)

Abby is 68 years old and has been married for 50 years. She has three kids, five grandchildren, and one great-grandchild. Abby's interview was a gift—a quiet spirit with a kind smile.

This Sassy Eve interview was so pleasant. Losing her mother at a young age, she spoke about her with delight. She is quiet in spirit and has only good things to say about everyone. She was funny and wanted to be with the Classy Eves, who are aged 70–79, because she liked their description. She will be there in two years. This pleasant Eve that I speak of now was not always like this.

From age eighteen to mid-thirties, she was on the wild side. Her story begins with her as a young follower, a role she recalls holding until she was about 15. She has four older siblings, and they were all leaders. Abby was never a leader; she told me she was young, dumb, and stupid. She was such a follower; the one who followed people. She would stand by, waiting for them to do something and then follow them. She finally began to change her mindset when she was 16 or 17. Then, at age 18, she got married. Women back then got married young. She did shock me. I knew in my mind that Abby, a Sassy Eve, went from 16–17, then married and did nothing wrong after that.

Not the case, she told me. I thought she was going to tell me she had a short window of temptation. Nope, she said she would go out partying, doing drugs, and she smoked weed (marijuana).

Growing up in Los Angeles, California, during the 1950s and 1960s, partying was the thing to do. Yes, they worked hard at their jobs. On the weekends, they enjoyed dancing and partying. Abby tried cocaine, but never got hooked on it. Of course, she drank liquor. I asked her if this was the period before she was married. No, she started during her marriage. It took her a minute to settle down. Saved and a Christian.

Her Serpent? Partying! (During that Period of Her Life, and She Knew Better.)

Sassy Eve: Michelle, Kia, Shelly, Sophia, Erica, Mindy, Abby, knows who she is. Sassy Eve Season: Walking in her purpose, she serves God and her community with Posie and Love. She is unapologetic, living for God and walking in his wisdom.

Connecting to Eve

Which Sassy Eve appealed to you?

Do you know any Eves with similar issues?

How would you support this Sassy Eve?

Classy Eve (70-79)

CHAPTER ELEVEN

CLASSY EVE (AGES 70–79) POISED, POWERFUL, AND FULL OF PEACE

"Since my youth, God, you have taught me, and to this day I declare your marvelous deeds. Even when I am old and gray, do not forsake me, my God, till I declare your power to the next generation, your mighty acts to all who are to come."

—Psalm 71:17–18 (NIV)

Classy Eve is still on assignment—still declaring God's goodness to the generations that follow.

She is poised, powerful, and full of peace. She enters a room with undeniable grace. Whether she walks with a cane, rides in a wheelchair, or strides freely, she captivates.

She's lived through decades of history, heartache, and hope—and it shows. Her face glows with peace, and her presence speaks of resilience. She trusts in God with everything she has, and nothing can shake her now.

Dina - Age 79, Divorced, Three Children, Five Grandchildren, Three Great-Grandchildren (Seen it All)

Dina is the embodiment of Classy Eve. Elegant, funny, and strong, she's seen it all—from historic events like the LA riots to the evolution of technology and society.

Her Serpent? Maintaining Her Cool. Patience!

She says she's mostly calm—until someone tries to take advantage of her. Then? She might forget she's a Christian for a moment.

"If the serpent came on a bad day?" she said, "I might just take a bite. The nerve of people!" Still, she always finds her way back to grace. Dina said she has lived through so many things in life that nothing shocks her anymore. God has allowed her to live all these years in her right, sound mind. She is healthy and whole; she never thought she would see all the years God has blessed her with, and she doesn't take life for granted. She still drives (of course, not on the freeway) and works part-time. Dina is a mix of warmth and fire, humor and holiness. Her life is a testimony to endurance, transformation, and unshakeable faith.

Precious – Age 75, Never married, Career Driven, (Forgiveness)

Precious is a vibrant 75-year-old woman. She has lived life her way—unapologetically. Throughout her life, she has learned a great deal, and wisdom is something she has gained. Now, at 75, she thanks the Lord for her life every day, grateful for His grace and mercy in allowing her to live with a sound mind.

Growing up in a family of 14 children, they were in church from a young age. She was also not allowed to visit other children's homes. They had to stay on their property and play there.

Precious also wants women to know she never had a desire to be married or have children. Witnessing various marriages and children brought her clarity on her life's path: to travel and support her family in any way possible. Precious provided spiritual and financial support to them. She has gone to more than 31 states and 26 countries. Precious believes that traveling and working have kept her busy and out of trouble, and she has quickly advanced in her job ranking.

Her Serpent? Unforgiving!

Precious states she has had a good life; the only thing she felt she fell short in was forgiveness. She allowed the serpent to attack her in forgiveness. It was hard for her to forgive people and let things go. Since she didn't know how to forgive people, she would just cut them off and not look back.

That's how it was in the past. It was a goodbye, and Precious was out. Even if the person apologized, she still wouldn't forgive them. She has lost some good friends over not forgiving. Forgiveness is something you have to work on, even if someone wrongs you. It is God's will to forgive everyone. You cannot be selective and choose who you want to forgive. You must forgive them all and have peace in your heart. She is almost there with forgiveness. It is something that she works on daily.

Janice – 74, Widowed, Married for 39 years (Still Standing)

She is a retired nurse. Janice married young and loved her husband; he was the absolute love of her life. They have three children and six grandchildren. Janice said she feels privileged that someone wants to know anything about her story. She grew up during a time when going outside to play was the only option for children, who were expected to be seen and not heard.

They started in a child's place. God first and respect were very important. Right now, she feels like she is blessed to be alive, but seeing family members and friends pass away has not been easy. Janice feels a little lonely without them.

Her Serpent? Jealousy! (In Her Past)

She thought she could not be a good mother to her children because she had to work. Janice would observe other parents with their children and admire their relationship, wishing to have something similar for her own family. For years, she thought that was the reason why she and her children were not close. She speaks to her children and grandchildren, but they seem uninterested in what she has to say. She recalls a time when her voice was the only one in the house, except for her husband's.

Her family is now surrounded by numerous outsiders and noise, as well as the constant presence of cell phones and social media.

Now that she is older, she sees that it wasn't about working a job, but about the time she invested with them. She did say that was her only regret in life. She wishes she could have figured out a way to manage quality time with them. She is no longer jealous of other parents. She's come to realize that everyone has a different story. Precious has always been a caregiver to others and cares deeply for her children. Her love for God tells her she is more than enough, and she has always been more than enough. Precious states she can no longer apologize for things she cannot change but grow from the mistakes of the past.

Edith – 72 years old, Married with One Child, Two Grandchildren (Cursed)

She loves that God has brought her this far in life, that she is still married to the man she didn't even know God had for her. There was a time in her life when Edith wasn't proud of herself; she allowed men to take advantage of her. Edith just wanted to be loved, she said.

Growing up, a family friend molested her; it may be the reason she was looking for love in men. She has since forgiven him and the life that is in her past. "Forgiveness has made me whole," she said. Edith knows that everything happens for a reason. She would not have met her husband if she hadn't taken the path of life that God put her on.

Edith said she also made mistakes, like having abortions, at least 9-10. If she can remember the number correctly, it was a lot. The reason for so many abortions was that the guys in her life at the time were not good men.

They were what you call bad boys or street guys. Edith believed they would not have made good fathers. She really thought they loved her until they showed her another side of themselves.

Her Serpent? Not Desiring of Love!

Later, Edith met this remarkable man, who was a faithful believer, and she had miscarriage after miscarriage. She told her husband she was cursed due to her history; he prayed with her, read the Bible with her, and they had one healthy baby.

Her husband told her to always walk in faith, as Proverbs 3:6 reminds us: *"In all your ways acknowledge him, and he shall direct thy paths."* It is her walk now.

For these three women: Dina, Precious, and Janice. Classy Eves are historical women who know life and how to navigate throughout with a peace and quietness about her, she need not say anything, time and history is her voice.

We should always thank and praise the women who have come before us, standing on their shoulders. I purpose in heart and mouth to always acknowledge them and thank them for wisdom and guidance.

Connecting to Eve

Which Classy Eve appealed to you?

Do you know any Eves with similar issues?

How would you support this Classy Eve?

Monarch Eve (80-99+)

MONARCH EVE (AGES 80–99+) WISDOM, GRACE, AND THE LEGACY OF FAITH

"Gray hair is a crown of glory; it is gained in a righteous life."
—Proverbs 16:31 (ESV)

Age is a badge of honor—especially when it reflects a life lived faithfully with God.

"There was also a prophet, Anna... She never left the temple but worshiped night and day, fasting and praying..."
—Paraphrased from Luke 2:36–38 (NIV)

Anna is the biblical model of the Monarch Eve—faithful, devoted, and still full of purpose in her elder years.

Monarch Eve has wisdom, grace, and the legacy of faith. The embodiment of elegance and wisdom. She has lived through decades of life's high and low-climbing hills, walking through peaks and valleys, standing firm in the midst of storms. Her strength is quiet, her presence calming, and her words full of seasoned truth.

She is graceful and poised, no longer rattled by the fleeting noise of the world. She thanks God daily for the gift of a sound mind, and for the peace that surpasses all understanding. Her faith has never wavered, only grown deeper.

Monarch Eve loves meaningful conversations and cherishes genuine connections with people of all ages. Despite her many personal losses, she remains full of joy and grounded in purpose. She is a living testimony of God's enduring faithfulness. With every breath, she preaches: God is good, God is faithful, and God is merciful.

Shirley – Age 83, Widow, Two Children, Three Grandchildren (Faithful)

Shirley was married to the love of her life for over 50 years. She misses him dearly and finds peace in the promise that she will see him again one day. When he became ill toward the end of their marriage, she was his caregiver—faithful to the very vow she made: in sickness and in health, until death do us part.

Now, Shirley is navigating a new season. She has had male friends and companions, but none compares to her husband. Instead of focusing on romance, she chooses to live an active and fulfilling life—traveling, going on cruises, and enjoying time with her children and grandchildren.

At this age, Shirley is confident that she would not eat the fruit. Even looking back, she says that while temptation may have crossed her mind, she never gave in.

"You wouldn't be human if you didn't think about getting even with someone or wanting to curse them out," she chuckles. "But we weren't raised that way."

She credits her upbringing for her discipline. Had she been raised in another era, she admits she might've had a wilder side. But growing up in the South and marrying young shaped her into the woman God called her to be. Rearing her children and living as a faithful wife became her calling.

That's not to say she didn't make mistakes, of course she did—but she understood the weight of disobedience. In her generation, stepping out of God's will be had serious, often dangerous, consequences. She recalls friends who ate the fruit and never recovered. Some were lost to violence or shameful acts. "It's better to walk with God," she says firmly.

Her serpents? Are all in her past. Now she walks in grace knowing God will bring her out of every situation!

Shirley lives by the truth of Psalm 37:4, *"Delight yourself in the Lord."* And she holds close Psalm 139:14,

"I will praise You, for I am fearfully and wonderfully made; marvelous are Your works, and that my soul knows very well."

Gail – Age 82, Widow, Four Children, Eight Grandchildren, Four Great-Grandchildren (Gracefully aging)

Without hesitation, Gail says she would never eat of the fruit—not then, and certainly not now.

Even as she deals with occasional forgetfulness in her older age, her faith remains intact. She knows right from wrong and has always leaned on her moral compass. Raised in a large Christian family with ten siblings, Gail grew up knowing what it meant to care for others. "Am I my brother's keeper? Absolutely," she says. That was the norm in her home.

Gail's parents lived well into their seventies, and their house was always full of uncles, cousins, nieces, nephews, someone was always around. Faith was the foundation of their family life. She learned early the importance of prayer and staying connected to God.

Her Serpent: Not understanding Discernment!

She was married young and believed in consulting her husband about everything. But she also learned that discernment doesn't come only from partnership; it comes from God.

Gail recalls a time early in her marriage when the serpent almost got her. She believed, mistakenly, that her husband had been unfaithful. The accusation nearly tore them apart. "If I had bitten into that fruit, if I had acted on that lie, I would've destroyed everything," Gail says.

Her anger almost pushed her toward violence. "I'm from Mississippi," she adds with a raised brow. "We wouldn't be having this conversation right now if I had followed through." Thankfully, it was a misunderstanding, and she found clarity before acting.

Her advice to every woman? "Trust God. He has the final say. Don't lean on your own understanding."

For Gail and Shirley: These women are women to be praised. They have lived beyond their years, peers, and family members. God has rewarded them as deserving servants.

Monarch Eve represents the final chapter of growth and glory on this side of eternity. She walks not just with experience—but with reverence. Her story isn't just about where she's been but how she finished well—a woman walking in wisdom, joy, and unwavering faith.

She is a pillar. She is a matriarch. She is a Monarch. As we visit this final chapter, let's always remember to be proud to stand on the shoulders of these awesome monarch Eves. More than God-fearing women, they are women of faith and resilience. Their eyes have seen many things; some are unspeakable, and they have walked in many lanes. Let's always honor and respect them.

We can learn from both the mistakes of the original Eve and the wisdom of today's Perfect Eves. Now, I pray the stories were enlightening and uplifting for you, and that your heart was opened to receive the wisdom they had to offer.

I pray we remain alert and at peace, discerning the serpent when he appears and seeking God's guidance every time he tries to deceive us. May we gather wisdom from every woman we meet—knowing that each story, no matter how big or small, holds a teachable moment. Every woman has a story. Let the Eves teach, inspire, and guide you.

Connecting to Eve

Which Monarch Eve appealed to you?

Do you know any Eves with similar issues?

How would you support this Monarch Eve?

CHAPTER THIRTEEN

A FINAL WORD TO EVERY EVE

Becoming the Eve God created you to be! I wasn't sure how to end this book at first. How do you close something so full of wisdom, pain, beauty, and truth? But as I reflected on the voices of the Eves who came before me, I realized: I don't need to have a perfect ending. What I need is gratitude.

From the stories of each Eve—from Youthful Eve to Monarch Eve—I've learned that there is power in taking pieces from every age and every experience to become the Eve that God has called me to be. I want pieces of every woman I've encountered. I want to take what I need to grow and pass that growth on to the next woman.

Some days, I may need the spice and grace of Classy Eve (age 70–79)—especially in the office or when facing challenges with poise. Other days, I might call on the energy and readiness of Woke and Enlightened Eve (age 40–49)—the one who says, "If you stay ready, you don't have to get ready."

There is an Eve who has walked through something I haven't yet, and their journeys have become tools in my toolbox, reminders that I can grow, adjust, and evolve. Their wisdom equips me. Their lessons refine me. Their victories inspire me. Even their struggles give me strength.

To Every Eve Reading This Book:

Be encouraged.

You are not the only one who has made mistakes.

You are not the only one who has eaten the fruit.

We all have.

No Eve is sinless. But each one has the power to rise again. Some of us took a bite yesterday, and others may have taken one years ago. Still, the stories of our lives prove that God's mercy is real and His grace is greater than our past.

Remember the wisdom of Scripture:

"Let the older women teach the younger women . . ."
—Titus 2:3–5

"As iron sharpens iron, so a friend sharpens a friend."
—Proverbs 27:17 (NLT)

Let this be a call: Let's become a haven for all Perfect Eves.

Let's build a safe space where hearts are sharpened like iron on iron—through mentorship, sisterhood, and wisdom that only comes from walking with the Lord.

Let the Generations Pour Into One Another

Let's create a place where:

- Faith is nurtured.

- Love is foundational.

- Growth is supported without judgment.

- The legacy of every Eve becomes a lifeline for the next.

I don't want to be a lost Eve, not to my family, not to my friends, and not to the women who need to hear my voice. I want to leave my footprints on this earth while I am still alive, walking in purpose and passing on everything I've learned.

I once saw a Facebook post from a woman saying, "When I get to heaven, I'm going to knock Eve out for what she did to all women." She went on to say how much she hated periods and labor pain. And honestly? In the past, I might've laughed along with her.

But now, I've learned better. I've made enough of my own mistakes that I imagine Eve might want to knock me out, too! We all fall short, and we are all learning. Let's give grace.

We Have More Resources Than Ever Before

The Eves of the past didn't have what we have now: Bible apps, podcasts, therapy, online sermons, digital communities, worship playlists, and mentors around every corner. We can search Scripture with a few keystrokes. We can find a sermon or devotion to help us through almost anything.

So let's use those resources, and let's use each other.

Let's set the example. Let's tell the younger Eves the truth: There is a serpent out there. He's real. He's clever. He's persistent.

But we serve a God who is wiser, stronger, and full of mercy.

A PRAYER
FOR EVERY EVE

My prayer for every Eve is:

- That you would grow.
- That you would know.
- That you would teach.
- That you would heal.
- That you would forgive.
- That you would shine.
- That you would walk with God every step of the way.

Exposure is the key to growth. The more we see, the more we know, and the more we can pass down. Our ancestors came from hardship. Monarch Eve may not have been a slave, but surely her mother or grandmother was. And now look at us: homeowners, leaders, healers, businesswomen, warriors of the Word.

Eve might have walked alone in the garden. But Perfect Eves don't have to walk alone anymore.

With knowledge comes responsibility. With grace comes power.

Let's rise together. Let's be Eve—redeemed.

ACKNOWLEDGMENTS

First, I want to thank God. He gave me the strength, courage, and peace I needed to keep going and finish this book. Without Him, none of this would be possible.

To my family—Michael, Kristian, Shannon, Marcus, and my granddaughter Keyani, thank you for loving me, supporting me, and giving me the space to follow this calling. Your patience and encouragement mean more than I can ever say.

To all my friends and sisters in Christ, Pastor Rodney & Lady Deborah, Bishop Tony & Lady Jackie Dunn, Sister Benita, Sister Josie, and to my Elders, Pastors, Ministers, and New Day church family who prayed for me and cheered me on, thank you. You reminded me that I wasn't alone, and you gave me the push I needed when I felt like giving up.

To everyone who worked on this book—my publisher, editor, designer, and all the behind-the-scenes helpers, thank you for sharing your gifts and helping me bring this vision to life.

And to you, the reader, thank you for picking up this book. My prayer is that it blesses you, gives you hope, and reminds you that your story matters, too.

ABOUT THE AUTHOR

Roshawn Burrell is a devoted follower of Christ, a Licensed Vocational Nurse, Medical Educator Consultant, with her MBA and project manager degree. An (LVN) instructor, minister, and hospitality leader with over 30 years of experience in healthcare. Rooted deeply in both nursing and ministry, she has dedicated her life to helping women move from fear to faith, anchoring themselves in the unshakable promises of God through every season.

Roshawn's journey of trusting God through uncertainty fuels her mission: to help others reclaim their identity, walk in spiritual strength, and rise with purpose. As an LVN instructor, she mentors with both compassion and conviction, blending practical wisdom with biblical truth. In her role as a church hospitality leader, she fosters safe, welcoming spaces where connection, healing, and sisterhood flourish.

She lives in Southern California, with her husband, Michael. They have three children, Kristian, Marcus, and Shannon, and her adult sister Cynthia, whom she lovingly cares for. Roshawn is a proud grandmother to Keyani. She fills her days with family laughter, heartfelt prayer, and the soulful sound of CeCe Winans, usually with cozy socks on and a heart full of gratitude.

Whether in the classroom, at church, or in the community, Roshawn's message is clear: Faith isn't just something we believe—it's how we live.

She invites you to join her on this journey, leaning into God's faithfulness, growing in spiritual strength, and walking boldly into the life He has promised.

Roshawn would love to hear how *The Perfect Eve* has touched your life. Please share with her at roshawnburrell@gmail.com.

www.ingramcontent.com/pod-product-compliance
Lightning Source LLC
Chambersburg PA
CBHW051212120626
46547CB00013B/1324